GUIDE TO

LAGO MAGGIORE

and the islands of the Golfo Borromeo

Texts by
Claudia Converso

Published by KINA ITALIA

V. Onsernone
Centovalli
Val Vigezzo
Valle Cannobina
Pzo. la Scheggia 2466
Cima d. Sassone 2086
Pzo. di Ruscada 2004
Mte. Loccia di Peve 2127
Piana di Vigezzo
Mosogno
Loco
Cavigliano
Tegna
Intragna
Losone
Locarno
Minusio
Gordola
Cugnasco
Brione
Borgnone
Camedo
Palagnedra
Toceno
Vocogno
Craveggia
Dissimo
Olgia
Folsogno
Albogno
Druogno
Re
Sta. Maria Maggiore
Orcesco
Malesco
Ascona
Lido di Ascona
Corona d. Pinci
Ronco
Fontana Martina
Magadino
Vira
Quartino
Brissago
S. Nazaro
Piazzogna
Gerra
S. Abbondio
Caviano
Pino
Indémini
Mte. Tamaro
Rivera
Bironico
Rocce d. Gridone 2063
Mte. Torriggia 1703
Mte. Limidario 2187
Mte. Zuccaro 1683
Pzo. Ragno 2289
La Cima 1810
Finero
Cúrsolo
Orasso
Gurro
Spoccia
S. Bartolomeo Valmara
Piággio di Valmara
Madonna di Ponte
Mte. Tógano 2299
Pzo. d. Diosi 2161
Riserva Naturale
Pzo. Mottác 1802
Cima d. Laurasca 2193
Cima Pedun 2111
Mte. Torrione 1984
La Piota 1925
Sólgia
Falmenta
Lunecco
Gurrone
Crealla
Socrággio
Cannóbio
Traffiume
Mte. Zeda 2156
Mte. Vadà 1836
Mte. Bavarione 1505
Mte. Spalavera 1534
Pzo. Marona 2051
Viggiona
Trárego
Carmine
Oggiogno
Cánnero Riviera
Veddasca
Biegno
Mte. Borgna
Armio
Curiglia
Maccagno
Agra
Mte. Gradisca 1057
Mte. Lema 1621
Dumenza
Sessa
Proman 2098
C. d'Alpino 1250
Pian Cavallone 1564
Cicogna
Nibbio
Béttola
Albo
Candóglia
Bráchio
Mergozzo
Piaggia
Scareno
Aurano
Intragna
Dónego
Barbè
Oggébbio
Gonte
Germignaga
Luino
Creva
Voldomino
Cremenaga
Mte. Mezzano
Ponte Tresa
Caslano
Lugano
Miazzina
Caprezzo
Esio
Novaglio
Pieggio
Unglasca
Cambiasca
Cossogno
Premeno
Pollino
Ghiffa
Porto Valtravaglia
Bédero
Brezzo di Bédero
Montegrino
Cadegliano
S. Bernardino
Verb.
Mte. Orfano
Trobaso
Vignone
Arizzano
Castelveccana
Nasca
Mesenzana
Grantola
Gugliate
Marchirolo
Fondotoce
Suna
Intra
Selasca
Feriolo
Pallanza
Verbánia
Laveno
Sasso del Ferro
Mte. di Colonna
Cassano Valcúvia
Ferrera
Cunardo
Marzio
Mte. Pianbello
Gravellona Toce
Baveno
Is. Borromee
Mte. Nudo
Cittíglio
Casalzuigno
Masciago Prim.
Bedero
Cuasso al Monte
Morcote
Mte. Zúchero
Stresa
Someraro
Cerro
Mombello
Leggiuno
Cúvio
Brinzio
Valganna
Ganna
Porto Cerésio
Omegna
Mottarone
Vezzo
Sangiano
Gemonio
Orino
Mte. Mártica
Mte. Legnone
Campo dei Fiori
Bisúschio
Viggiú
Mte. Pravello
Besano
Mte. Mazzarone
Gignese
Magognino
Carpugnino
Cardana
Caldana
Trevisago
Rasa di Varese
Arcisate
Clivio
Rancate
Stabio
Agrano
Mte. d. Falò
Brovello-Carpugnino
Monvalle
Besozzo
Olginasio
Cócquio-Trevisago
Gavirate
Velate
Barasso
Luvinate
Induno Olona
Brenno Useria
Pratolungo
Armeno
Mte. Cornaggia
Belgirate
Lesa
Bardello
Comério
Casciago
Masnago
Ambrogio
Varese
Rodero
Uggiate
Orta
Massino Visconti
Nebbiuno
Brebbia
Malgesso
Bregano
Biandronno
Morosolo
Cantello
Valmorea
Fosseno
Sólcio
Ispra
Travedona
Calcinate d. P.
Bobbiate
Malnate
Cagno
Méina
Quassa
Monate
Cadrezzate
Osmate
Cazzago Brábbia
Bodio Lomnago
Capolago
Inarzo
Galliate Lomb.
Azzate
Bizzozero
Binago
Ghevio
Dagnente
Angera
Comabbio
Lentate Verb.
Varano Borghi
Casale Litta
Daverio
Brunello
Gazzada Schianno
Morazzone
Lozza
Vedano Olona
Beregazzo
Bolzano Nov.
Invório
Oleggio Castello
Arona
Taino
Mercallo
Crósio d. V.
Caidate
Castiglione Olona
Castelnuovo Bozzente
Gozzano
Paruzzaro
Mercurago
Lisanza
Corgeno
Villadósia
Mornago
Sumirago
Montonate
Castronno
Caronno Var.
Oltrona S. Mamette
Venegono Sup.
Barquedo
Briga Novarese
Talonno
Dormelletto
Oriano Ticino
S. Anna
Sesto Calende
Cuvirone
Cimbro
Vergiate
Quinzano S. Pietro
Albizzate
Solbiate Arno
Carnago
Gornate Sup.
S. Bartolomeo
Appiano Gentile
Gargallo
Maggiate
Rotta
Comignago
Castelletto Sopra Ticino
Sesona
Ierago
Oggiona S. Stéfano
Caiello
Castel Seprio
Tradate
Veniano
Borgomanero
Gattico
Campagnola
Dorbiè
Golasecca
Besnate
Orago
Cavária
Premezzo
Jerago
Peve ranza
Lonate Ceppino
Abbiate Guazzone
Lurago Marinone
Sta. Croce
Vergano Nov.
Veruno
Revislate
Borgo Ticino
Somma Lombardo
Arsago Sépirio
Bolladello
Cedrate
Bérgoro
Sárrate
Locate Var.
Carbonate
Sta. Cristina
Cureggio
Agrate
Gagnago
Contúrbia
Coarezza
Boca
Bogogno
Marzalesco
Varallo Pombia
Casorate Sempione
Crenna
Cassano Magnago
Fagnano Ol.
Mozzate
Gallarate

Isola Bella at sunset

INTRODUCTION

GEOGRAPHICAL INFORMATION

The origins of Lake Maggiore, also known as Lake Verbano, are found in water erosion which, through the action of the ice, led to the formation of the basin. It is Italy's second largest lake after Lake Garda, with a 212 cm² surface extending to a length of around 66 km and a breadth ranging from 2 km (between Arona and Angera) and 4.3 km between Cannero and Germignana. Its average depth is 175 m, its deepest point 372 m. Geographically and administratively speaking, the territory is split between three regions - Lombardy, Piedmont and Switzerland. The three areas also offer widely differing landscapes. To the north, there are the immense alluvial plains formed by the Ticino and the Maggia, which extend into the chains of the Val Maggia and the Val Verzasca and the Magadino Plain, once marshland. To the east, there is Mount Tamaro (1967 m) and the foothills of the Alps (Gambarogno, 1739 m). Further south, past the Val Travaglia, there is Sasso del Ferro (1062 m), lying behind Laveno, where the coastline starts as sheer cliff-face but becomes less steep further on. To the south, there is flat ground, bordered by the Ticino Nature Park on the eastern side and the Lagoni di Mercurago Nature Park, a typically marshy area, on the western side. The Vergante area covers a large portion of the western edge, running from Arona to Feriolo. This area is characterized by high ground (hillocks) which rarely exceed 800 m in altitude. Further north, the granite Mount Mottarone (1491 m) marks the natural boundary between Lake Maggiore and Lake d'Orta and Mount Orfano (794 m) separates Lake Maggiore from the smaller Lake Mergozzo. North of Punta Castagnola (from which the summits of the Alps and Monte Rosa can be seen), Monte Zeda (2156 m) towers over the lake.
The lake's main tributary is the Ticino, which flows north-east after crossing the Magadino plain and out to the south, as the only outlet, near Sesto Calende. Other tributaries include the rivers Maggia and Verzasca to the north, the rivers Giona, Tresa, Boesio and Bardello to the east and the rivers Erno, Toce, S. Bernardino and Cannobino to the west.

THE GULF OF BORROMEO

On the western side, the lake turns inwards by the Toce valley to form the enchanting Gulf of Borromeo. The so-called Borromean Islands (Isola Madre, Isola Bella, Isola dei Pescatori, also called Superiore, and Isola S. Giovanni) lie here.

CLIMATE

The area is celebrated for its mild climate, with average winter temperatures between 3-7°C and average summer temperatures of 22°C. Rainfall is particularly heavy (around 1,500 mm a year), due to the geographical position of the lake, and Spring is the rainy season. Typical winds are breezes, including the "tramontana" (north wind), the south wind, the Lake Maggiore wind (which causes storms), the "cüss" (coming from Lake d'Orta) and other more localized winds, such as the "marenca" (over Intra) and the "mergozzo" (from the west over the Gulf of Borromeo).

FLORA AND FAUNA

Only a small part of the woodland which once covered the area remains. This includes conifers, birch trees, beech trees, chestnuts, oak trees, elms, locust trees and flowering plants. Various fruit trees are cultivated, including orange, lemon and olive trees, thanks to the mild climate. Reeds, sedge, iris and waterlilies grow in the marshy area, together with many other plant species typical to this type of habitat. The area is also notable for its gardens, parks and botanical gardens, renowned for their beauty and the presence of rare and exotic plants (Villa Pallavicino, Villa Taranto, Isola Madre, Isola Bella). The highly varying types of fauna found there reflect the geographical variety of the area and almost all species typical of the habitats described can be seen. The lake is also home to a variety of lake-dwelling fish (chub, eel, whitefish, pike and trout).

HISTORY

The area was already inhabited in the Iron Age and was to come first under Gaulish, then Roman rule. The Romans created the settlements of Angera and Lucerne (the principal commercial and military centers) here and gave the inhabitants of the area Roman citizenship in the year 45 BC. The area passed into the hands of the Longobards in the early VI century, the Franks (who divided it into the counties of Angera, Seprio and Ossola) in the second half of the century and finally to the Ottos. From the XII century, a number of families ruled the area in succession, including the Torriani family of Como, who waged war with the Visconti for many years and were conquered by them in 1227. The latter's predominance continued until 1439, when Arona passed to the Borromeo family. The predominance of this family started in 1441 and continued even during the period of Spanish domination (1535-1706), the time at which such renowned family members as San Carlo and Cardinal Federico were born. The Treaties of Utrecht and Rastadt (1713 and 1714) marked the passing of the area under Hapsburg rule. The Treaty of Worms and the Peace Treaty of Aquisgrana gave the Piedmontese side to the Kings of Sardinia and confirmed the Swiss ownership of the northern part. The part in Lombardy remained in Austrian hands until 1859, with two brief interruptions marked by the setting up of the Cisalpine Republic (1797) and the Kingdom of Italy (1805) by desire of Napoleon.

ART

There is little trace remaining of prehistoric and Roman settlements, although it is known that numerous monuments and churches were erected on the ruins of buildings from the latter era. Numerous examples of Romanesque architecture remain, with an enchanting mix between the canonical style and the traditional architectures of the region. The Renaissance and Baroque periods saw the building of churches and aristocratic buildings surrounded by magnificent parks and gardens. The large villas and parks which today form a multicolored array of different architectural styles (Liberty, Neoclassical, Baroque and Renaissance) around the edge of the lake were built in the eighteenth and nineteenth centuries and blend perfectly into the magnificent landscape around them.

ARONA

The largest town on the southern bank of the lake, Arona is an important commercial and tourist centre looking out over Fort Angera and the lakeside gardens, trees and houses. The area was inhabited as early as the tenth century and saw a sudden population boom in 1162, when it became the destination of refugees from Milan after the city was destroyed by Barbarossa. From 1439 until the end of the eighteenth century, it was the domain of the Borromeo family. It was the birthplace of San Carlo Borromeo (1538-1584), to whom a monument known as the Sancarlun is dedicated. The town contains the ancient Romanesque Church of SS. Martiri Graziano e Felino, which has several times been restored over the centuries: in its interior (1800) visitors can admire some remarkable sixteenth-century stained glass windows (by Palma the Younger and Bergognone). Only a short distance away stands the collegiate church of S. Maria Nascente: built between the fifteenth and seventeenth centuries, its façade is decorated with a fine marble portal surmounted by an elegant rose-window. The partly Romanesque (lower part) and partly Gothic (upper part) bell-tower originally belonged to the Church of SS. Martiri. The interior contains a precious poliptych (1511) by Gaudenzio Ferrari. The fifteenth-century Casa del Podestà (or Palace of Justice) looks out over the Piazza del Popolo and has a fine portico decorated with tondi and terra cotta busts. The same square is the site of the Church of the Madonna di Piazza (also known as the Church of S. Maria di Loreto) which was built in 1592 and contains an imitation of the Sanctuary of Loreto. The remains of the so-called Fort Viscontea are to be seen on the hill of Arona. It probably dates back to the thirteenth century and, like Fort Angera, was the scene of fierce fighting between the Visconti and Torriani families. The building eventually became the Borromeo residence but was destroyed on the orders of Napoleon in 1800. Arona is also active from a cultural

1) Collegiate church of S. Maria, central nave
2)View of the church of "Natività di Maria Vergine", bell-tower

3 

4 

3) "Virgin Protectress of Navigators" by P. Negri. Background: Rocca d'Angera
4) Court of Justice (15th cent.)
5) Lakeside and Rocca Viscontea
6) Corso Repubblica, with Rocca di Angera in the background

5 

6 

point of view: besides offering the magnificent gardens of the Villa Cantoni, it is the annual site of an important organ festival, as well as prestigious art exhibitions and an antiques market, which is held every month in the splendid setting of Piazza del Popolo.

THE SAN CARLONE MONUMENT

On reaching the town from the lake, the first sight you see is almost certainly the San Carlone, a huge copper statue (35 metres high, including the granite pedestal). It stands on the hill behind the town on which the remains of Fort Viscontea also lie. Designed in 1614 by Giovan Battista Crespi, called Il Cerone, it was only finished in 1698, almost a century after the canonization of San Carlo Borromeo, to whom it is dedicated. The monument, which was to be made of marble, was commissioned by Marco Aurelio Grattarola and Cardinal Federico Borromeo, cousin of the saint and Archbishop of Milan. It shows the bareheaded saint in the act of benediction: his right hand is raised, while his left hand clutches the text of the Council of Trent. At the feet of the saint is a terrace with steps leading into the statue. These lead right up into its head, from which you can enjoy a remarkable panoramic view. The square opposite the statue is the site of a Baroque church dedicated to the saint: a nineteenth-century stairway leads inside to the cupola, decorated with eighteenth-century frescoes and the reconstruction of the so-called "room of the three lakes". The original of this is situated in Fort San Carlo, where the saint was born. The original furnishings were moved into the church in 1800 when Napoleon ordered the destruction of the Visconti building. The San Carlo seminary (1620-1643), to the left of the statue, is today used as a college.

1) Portrait of S. Carlo Borromeo
2) S. Carlo Seminary, dominated by the famous "S. Carlone" statue
3) The copper "colossus" of S. Carlo

S. CARLO BORROMEO
Copper statue erected in 1624
in Arona (Lake Maggiore)
Measurements
Total height 35.00 metres
Statue 23.40 »
Plinth 11.70 »
Around the Head 6.50 »
Length of the Face 2.40 »
Length of the Nose 0.85 »
Length of the Ear 0.75 »
Width of the Eye 0.50 »
Width of the Mouth 0.75 »
Length of the Arm 9.10 »
Length of the Breviary 4.20 »
Width of the Hand 1.45 »
Length of the Thumb 1.40 »
Circumference of the Thumb 1.00 »
Length of the Forefinger 1.95

1) Aerial view
2) Panorama
3) Solcio

MEINA

Situated on the road leading from Arona to Stresa, this town stands in a beautiful spot at the mouth of the river Tiasca. It lies partly along the tree-covered hill of Dagnente and partly along the banks of the lake. It was the site of a human settlement as far back as the Bronze Age and is mentioned in Mediaeval times as Madina. Like many other areas of Lago Maggiore, it first belonged to the archbishopric of Milan; it then passed into the hands of the Visconti and in 1440 fell into the possession of the Borromeo family. The ancient town centre is still crossed by little cobbled streets leading to the old houses. From the sixteenth century, a flourishing wood and coal trade developed between Meina and Milan. The Town Hall preserves a nineteenth-century fresco, while numerous eighteenth and nineteenth-century villas still testify to the popularity of Meina in past centuries. Villa Favorita was built around 1850 and constitutes a harmonious blend of severe Neo-classical and early Art Nouveau architectural styles. However, the most interesting residence is Villa Faraggiana. Built in late Neo-Classical style, its grandiose façade - decorated with a Neo-Classical timpanum and embellished with stuccoes - is reflected in the lake which it overlooks. The villa is immersed in a lush garden-park abloom with magnolias, camelias, azaleas and many other species of trees and plants.

1

2

3

LESA

Lesa is situated on the west bank of the lake directly opposite Ispra. Its particularly mild climate is due to the protection of Mount San Salvatore (794 m) and Mount Cornaggia (922 m), which lie behind it. The land on which the town lies was formed by the deposits left over the centuries by the river Erno, which flows into the lake a few kilometres to the south. During the Middle Ages it was the site of the Lombard and Frank courts and also the court of justice of the Archbishop of Milan. In 1441, it became the domain of the Borromeo family, to whom it was conceded by the Visconti. Lesa was much-loved by Cavour and a favourite haunt of Alessandro Manzoni, and it was here that the writer Giulio Carcano died in 1882. The Romanesque church of S. Sebastiano (eleventh century) and the church of S. Giorgio (Villa Lesa), with a five-tiered Romanesque bell-tower and a Crucifixion (1500) attributed to Giovanni da Lumo, are among the oldest buildings. Lying along the lakeside are the Neo-Gothic Villa Tadini, with its fine Art Nouveau railings, and Palazzo Stampa, which once belonged to Manzoni's second wife and is now a history museum. Its beautiful gardens at one time stretched right down to the lake. Among the numerous eighteenth-nineteenth century residences is Villa Nosada, built in eighteenth-century Neo-Classical style with nineteenth-century modifications. Lesa is an excellent departure point for a trip to the Alto Vergante. Only three kilometres from the town is Comnago, from which point you can reach Monte delle Croce on foot and enjoy a unique panoramic view over and around the lake.

1) Church of S. Sebastiano
2) Lakeside and landing stage

1

BELGIRATE

Belgirate stands at the foot of Motta Rossa, a point offering a wide panorama over the lake and mountains. The town is as well known for its extremely mild climate as for its constantly sunlit position. Its name seems to originate from its geographical position at a point where the coast curves slightly to the west to form the bay of the Borromean Islands. Belgirate was also a renowned tourist spot in the past, its climate and beauty having enchanted illustrious figures such as Niccolò Tommaseo, Garibaldi, Manzoni, Verga, De Amicis and D'Annunzio. It was also the setting for a famous passage in Stendhal's Chartreuse de Parme. Treves, the publisher, hosted in his villa famous writers and poets who were to produce some of the finest nineteenth and 20th century literature: Guido Gozzano indelibly linked the name of the town with his work by making Villa Carlotta the setting for L'Amica di Nonna Speranza. This is a superb building dating back to last century and its famous garden contains trees planted centuries ago.

The ancient village centre is made up of characteristic narrow streets rising up between old houses, many of which are embellished with elegant porticoes. The nearby Gothic church of S. Marta contains fifteenth-century frescoes. On the outskirts are large villas immersed in luxuriant gardens. About four kilometres away is Massino Visconti, which is believed to be the place of origin of the Visconti family, who were for long resident in the castle which can still be seen today.

1) Picturesque view
2) 13th cent. church and Romanesque bell-tower

3

4

5

3) Aerial view
4) Harbour
5) Lakeside promenade

1) Golfo Borromeo
2) The "Lido". Stresa-Mottarone cable car terminus.
3) Hotels seen from the lake
4) Sunset on the lake

STRESA

The town is situated at the extreme southern point of the Golfo Borromeo in a splendid woodland setting on the slopes of Mount Mottarone and is perhaps the most famous holiday resort in the Lago Maggiore region. Known during the first millennium as Strixia, this ancient fishing village became the feudal domain of the Visconti in the fifteenth century and later passed into the hands of the Borromeo family. The tourist attraction gained impetus with the arrival of English and North European visitors (most notably Stendhal, Dickens and Byron), who stayed in Stresa during their Grand Tour and wrote highly romantic descriptions of the area. The construction of the coast road, ordered by Napoleon at the beginning of the nineteenth century, and the inauguration in 1911 of the Stresa-Mottarone electric rack railway (closed in 1964 and replaced by a funicular railway in 1970) gave a further boost to tourism. The increased construction of villas and other buildings, which began towards the end of the eighteenth century, continued during the nineteenth and early twentieth centuries. The most prestigious lakeside hotels were built between the late nineteenth and early twentieth centuries: all are set amidst luxuriant parks

1

2

4

and gardens (Hôtel des Iles Boromées, Regina Palace), and villas - almost all of which have been turned into hotels. And yet Stresa has not rested on its past glories but has adapted to the new tourism by becoming an important centre for literary prizes, musical events and congresses. Celebrated for its aristocratic residences - including the nineteenth-century Villa Vignol (once belonging to Italo Balbo), Villa Niobe and the well-known Villa Pallavicino (see below) - Stresa has a splendid lakeside area overlooked by Piazza Marconi and the parish church of S. Ambrogio. Rebuilt in 1790, the central-plan church preserves some fine sixteenth-seventeenth century canvases. Behind the church is Villa Ducale (1770), once known as Palazzo Bolongaro. In 1848, the gardened residence was given by Anna Maria Bolongaro to Antonio Rosmino, the philosopher, who spent the last years of his life there and died in 1855. Bought by the Duchess of Genoa in 1857, the villa is today the International Rosminian Study Centre and a museum dedicated to the philosopher. The Collegio Rosmini, on the road to Mottarone, houses a prestigious art collection, while the church of SS. Crocefisso, situated at the side of the college, is home to the memorial monument to Rosmini (1859). In the town itself, the modern Palazzo dei Congressi plays host to numerous conventions as well as to the famous Stresa Music Week festivals, with the participation of internationally famous artists every year. Not far away is Piazza Cadorna, which stands in a setting of elegant porticoed buildings and is always bustling with tourists who come to visit the shops there.

Boats for excursions to the Borromean Islands leave from Piazza Marconi.

1

1) Stresa and the Golfo Borromeo, with Isola Bella

2
Motta
3
4
5

1) The Golfo Borromeo islands
2) Night view
3) Fireworks over the lake
4) Fountain in the public gardens and Hotel Regina
5) "La Sirenetta"

VILLA PALLAVICINO

Just outside Stresa, on the lakeside road going south-east, stands Villa Pallavicino, a Neo-Classical residence built in Ligurian style. It is situated in a large park which was opened to the public in 1956. The villa was built in 1855 for Ruggero Bonghi, a statesman, and later became the property first of the Duke of Vallombrosa and then of Pallavicino, the Italian marquis from whom it takes its name. The park was gradually restyled and enlarged by successive owners. Standing only fifty metres from the edge of the lake, the building rises to a height of about twenty metres above water level and is separated from the lake by a terraced garden in classic English style. The park contains wide, shady paths and large flower beds, and surrounds the villa completely. The lawn occupies a large, slightly sloping surface and is crowned by a line of centuries-old trees and a wood with a natural brook running through it. The upper part of the park takes on a more formal appearance as it opens out onto a terraced garden after the Italian style. It is decorated with large geometrical beds of extremely colourful and varied flowers and a splendid rose garden, all of which are set off by stone ornaments and large vases. The huge garden is also home to a private zoo: its large enclosures hold ostriches, kangaroos, llamas and other more or less exotic animals.

1) Lake
2) Garden and fountain
3) Exterior view of villa

MOTTARONE

1

Mount Mottarone, a 1491-metre granite mass, divides the Lago Maggiore and Lago d'Orta areas. It already attracted many visitors last century, English travellers in particular, who would depart from the lakeside resorts where they were staying and make their way up to the peak. In 1911, the mountain was connected to Stresa by a rack railway, which was closed in 1964 and replaced in 1970 by a funicular railway. Instead of following the route used by cars to reach almost the top of the mountain, this railway gives visitors access to the slopes. A cross was erected on the summit in 1952, and from this point one can enjoy a splendid panorama, taking in the area from Monte Rosa to Monviso: in the distance on very clear days one can even see the Apennines, Lago Maggiore, Lago d'Orta, Mergozzo, Varese, Monate and other valleys in Lombardy. On the Lago Maggiore side of the mountain, the panorama takes in the vast area of Borromeo Park. This is crossed by a road (cars must pay a toll fee) which runs through woods filled with pines, beeches and chestnut trees and dwellings typical of mountain and marsh areas. Mount Mottarone, which is also famous for its ski resorts and beautiful pistes, can be reached from Stresa by passing through Gignese, a charming holiday resort at an altitude of 700 metres and famous for its umbrella museum. Opened in 1939, it remains the only one in Europe.
Numerous umbrellas and parasols dating from the nineteenth century to the present day are exhibited there, bearing witness both to the work of local umbrella manufacturers and to the evolution of umbrella styles.
After the Alpine resort of Gignese come the botanical gardens of Alpinia, containing Alpine medicinal flowers. From this point, the visitor can enjoy a most beautiful panorama over Lago Maggiore, the Borromean Islands and the Swiss Alps.

2

1) Stresa-Mottarone cable way
2) Gignese - Umbrella Museum; silk parasol (1870)
3) Ski slopes; background: Monte Rosa chain

3

ISOLA BELLA

Isola Bella is situated about 400 metres from the lakeside of Stresa and rises just 28 metres above water level at its highest point. North-East of the Isola dei Pescatori, it is certainly the most important of the Borromean islands, because of its splendid Baroque house and the charming garden it stands in. The island was originally inhabited by fishermen, and it was here that Carlo Borromeo III (1586-1652) decided to build an entire town, which he wished to name after his wife, Isabella d'Adda - hence the present name of the island. Work on transforming the island and building the house began in 1632 and continued in earnest under the supervision of the son of Carlo III, Vitaliano Borromeo VI (1620-1690), who also decided to create the garden and commissioned completion of the house to Angelo Crivelli, who was later helped by a number of famous contemporary architects. The monumental Baroque-style complex was enlarged during the eighteenth and nineteenth centuries, while the northern façade was only completed in 1959.

The homogeneous construction is formed by three large but compact masses: the central one has four floors, while the side ones have only three. It was in this residence on April 14th, 1935 that a meeting took place between representatives of the Italian, French and British governments (Mussolini, Laval and MacDonald), with the aim of establishing peace in Europe by means of a cooperation agreement between the three countries. In the courtyard, which stands to the right of the complex, is the Borromeo chapel - designed at

1) Borromeo family arms
2) Aerial view

3) Harbour

4) Indian peacock in the island gardens

the end of the eighteenth century but only built in the second half of the nineteenth century. The chapel contains a funeral monument to the Birago family (sculpted in 1522 by Agostino Busti and known as "Il Bambaia") as well as monuments to Giovanni and Camillo Borromeo (sculpted by Giovanni Antonio Amadeo). The first and second were brought to the chapel from the church of S. Francesco Grande in Milan, while the third was originally in the church of S. Pietro in Gessate.

The garden is one of the most remarkable from the Italian seventeenth-century Baroque period. It was designed by Angelo Crivelli and Carlo Fontana and built at the same time as the house. The garden is arranged asymmetrically with respect to the house itself and is formed by ten tiered terraces, decorated with fountains, statues (mostly sculpted by Simonetta and Resnati) and niches. The splendid plant life includes rhododendrons, azaleas, a wide variety of camelias, as well as orange trees, cedars, magnolias and many other exotic species, each of which bears a label showing its origin and name. On the highest terrace stands the "Theatre", an amphitheatre built on a stone base decorated with the coats-of-arms of the Borromeo family. The upper part symbolizes the triumph of the family house, showing a unicorn rampant with the Ticino and the Tosa - two tributaries of the lake - at its feet. In front of the amphitheatre stands a splendid garden with a magnificent view out over the lake.

1) Island seen from lakeside
2) Palazzo Borromeo at night
3) Back-lighted Statues in the terraced gardens

1) Island and Monte Sasso di Ferro
2) Terraced gardens and Belvedere tower

3) Entrance to the "Giardino dell'Amore"
4) Amphitheatre overlooking gardens and statues, the most important of which is the Unicorn

1

2

1) Steps to terraced gardens, statues and obelisks
2) Amphitheatre avenue
3) Gardens seen from above
4) English style flower garden
5) Unicorn, symbol of the Borromeo family

3

4

5

PALAZZO BORROMEO: THE INTERIOR

Like the island, the house is open to visitors from the middle of March to the end of October. It is sumptuously furnished and contains fine tapestries and arrases, as well as valuable paintings (by Bramantino, Beltraffio, Carracci, Gaudenzio Ferrari, Luca Giordano, Macrino d'Alba, Paris Bordon, Paolo Veronese, Tiepolo, Zuccarelli and others). If you go up the staircase to the first floor, you can admire the banquetting hall, the conference room (which hosted the meeting between Mussolini, Laval and MacDonald in 1935) and the Napoleon Room (where the emperor stayed). Then there is the ballroom (1794-95) designed by Zanoia and the arras gallery, containing precious seventeenth-century Flemish works. A spiral staircase leads down to the underground rooms - six man-made grottoes with mosaic walls. These contain statues from all periods and places, prehistoric objects and an iron-age pirogue discovered near Ispra.

1) Throne Room of Carlo Borromeo IV, with 18th cent. furnishings
2) Music and Conference Room
3) Arras Gallery; entrance to gardens in the background
4) The "Great Hall" designed by Richini for special occasions
5) Sixth grotto, with a model of the Isola Bella ▶▶
6) Fifth grotto, with funeral urns and remains of the metropolis of Golasecca (1,000-400 BC) ▶▶
7) Mosaic table, a present from Pope Leo XII to Count Gilberto Borromeo, Extraordinary Ambassador of the Emperor Francis Joseph to the Holy See. ▶▶

ISOLA DEI PESCATORI

Separated from Isola Bella by a small island called La Marghera, the Isola dei Pescatori can be reached on foot from the other islands when the water level drops. It is about 300 metres in length and 100 metres in width. Also known as Isola Superiore, it is distinguished from the other two main islands of the Borromean group, Isola Bella and Isola Madre, by the lack of the aristocratic houses and gardens which represent the main attraction of the other islands. The small village situated on Isola dei Pescatori is today still inhabited by fishermen and keeps the charming beauty characteristic of villages in the area. The elegant dwellings are almost completely white but are set off by coloured framework, wooden porches and stone portals. They stand very close to one another and are separated by narrow archways. The picturesque complex is crossed by small winding streets which intersect the long, narrow central road along which most of the shops are situated.
The island was once part of the parish of Baveno and still contains land belonging to the monks of Scozzola from the Abbey of S. Donato a Sesto Calende. It was on this land that, perhaps as early as the 10th century, the friars built a chapel dedicated to San Gandolfo, the Christian martyr. Later restructured and transformed into a parish church, the building was dedicated to San Vittore in 1627 and underwent several successive restorations. Of the ancient Romanesque chapel, only the apse remains: this corresponds to the present left-hand chapel, which is decorated with three blind arches and brickwork.

1) Isola dei Pescatori at sunset

1

2

1) Dream panorama
2) Typical fishing boats in the harbour
3) Picturesque view
4) Lakeside view

3

4

Until quite recently, not all of the island had been built on. The first population increase occurred in the fifteenth century, when many came there to seek refuge from wars, invasions and the plague epidemics which were then raging throughout the hinterland. But the greatest population increase took place between the late sixteenth and the early seventeenth centuries, when most of the inhabitants of Isola Bella moved there. This was the period in which Carlo Borromeo III and his son Vitaliano VI decided to build the luxurious family residence and the magnificent park, which required large-scale transformation and restyling work. Only very few of the present population are fishermen, for most are involved in tourist and restaurant activities. However, the spectacle of the typical fishing boats, with their bell-shaped sails supported by iron stays, as they set out at dawn to cast their nets is still one of the main attractions of an island that was much-loved by nineteenth-century Lombard landscape artists such as Filippo Carcano and Mosè Bianchi.

1

1) Romantic lake excursion; Isola dei Pescatori and Isola Bella in the background

BAVENO

Thanks to its proximity to Stresa and the Islands, Baveno has become an important holiday resort (with newly built hotels such as the Hotel Dino, with 375 rooms and 800 beds).
From the beautiful lakeside facing Isola dei Pescatori, you can walk up to the town and visit the church of SS. Protasio e Gervasio (fifth century) with its Romanesque bell-tower and façade (twelfth century) bearing a dedication to the Emperor Claudius. The octagonal baptistery contains fifteenth-sixteenth century frescoes. The small votary chapel was erected in 1630 to mark liberation from the plague. Casa Morandi is an eighteenth-century house with an external stairway. Just outside the town stands Villa Branca (originally Villa Henfrey, 1844), an English-style residence which hosted Byron, Queen Victoria, Churchill and other celebrated figures. Baveno is famous for its pink granite, which was used to build the Galleria Vittorio Emanuele in Milan.

1) Stonemasons' monument
2) Church of S. Gervaso e S. Protaso, bell-tower
3) Lakeside
4) Lake and landing stage
5) Church of S. Gervaso e S. Protaso
6) "Casa Morandi" (national monument)

1) Lakeside and Monte Orfano
2) Camping sites

FERIOLO

Situated at the western-most end of the Golfo Borromeo, close to the mouth of the river Toce, Feriolo is a well-appointed tourist resort. It is particularly popular because of its lakeside scenery and characteristic houses, which have helped it to preserve the appearance of the typical fishing village it used to be. Known in ancient times as Forum Juli, the picturesque village has on two occasions been completely submerged by the swollen waters of the lake (in 1867 and 1885). Although it is not of particular interest from an artistic point of view, Feriolo attracts many visitors who use it as a departure point for climbing to the top of Monte Camoscio, which offers a splendid panorama over the lake, or Monte Orfano, which is famous for its white granite quarries and offers a splendid view of Lago di Mergozzo.

2

FONDOTOCE

1) Panorama

Fondotoce lies on the road leading from Feriolo to Pallanza. The village is situated next to the tributary of nearby Lago di Mergozzo. Once linked to Lago Maggiore, Lago di Mergozzo was gradually separated over the centuries by the alluvial deposits of the river Toce, which runs into the basin a few kilometres to the south. The village has preserved the nineteenth-century parish church of the Vergine Addolorata, which has a single nave and a semi-circular apse. On the outskirts of the village is the oratory of S. Giacomo al Basso, a Romanesque building in rustic style dating back to the year 1100. It stands in an isolated position and was built of rocks and large blocks of river stone. Apart from these two buildings, the main attractions of Fondotoce are its typical lakeside village atmosphere and the natural environment that surrounds it. The WWF has recently created a protected area in the beautiful local canebrake where one can admire the typical flora and fauna of the region. Not far from Fondotoce, in the immediate hinterland, stands Bieno, a mountain spot once famous for the numerous madonnas painted on the walls of its houses. Here you can visit the beautiful church of S. Maria, which dates back at least to the twelfth century. Like most of the local churches it was built with a mixture of materials (pebbles and blocks of stone).

1) Church of S. Giovanni Battista

MONTORFANO

Monte Orfano [Mount Orphan] (794 m) is so called because it stands by itself (orfano = orphan) in the vicinity of Lago di Mergozzo, a lake once connected to Lago Maggiore and particularly well known to fishing enthusiasts. Lying on the slopes of Monte Orfano, Montorfano is a picturesque village with old stone houses. It also preserves one of the most beautiful churches in the region, the church of S. Giovanni, a Lombard Romanesque building probably erected in the twelfth century and built almost entirely of granite quarried from Monte Orfano. Its interior is unique among local churches because of its cross-plan, and its octagonal cupola rests on conical pendentives. It also has a rare baptismal font dating back to the early Christian era. The foundations of an earlier church have been uncovered to one side of the altar.

VILLA TARANTO

This villa was built in 1875 by Conte Orsetti and is set amidst a park of about 20 hectares, considered to be the finest botanical garden in Italy. The property was bought in 1931 by a Scotsman, Neil McEacharn, and later donated to the Italian state. McEacharn radically transformed it into an English-style botanical garden containing one of the richest collections of exotic plants in Europe. He also created a small valley (full of fine magnolias), built the bridge to one side of the front lawn and levelled out a rise in order to install the lotus pond and picturesque stairway. After admiring avenues, lawns, terraced gardens, waterfalls, fountains and ponds (near one of which stands Vincenzo Gemito's famous "Pescatore", a statue of a Neapolitan street urchin), you come to the fir grove and flower-beds full of multi-coloured herbaceous plants and dahlias. The splendid greenhouse (called the winter garden) contains heated ponds full of wonderful varieties of lilies; there are also Japanese maples, rhododendrons, a charming magnolia corner, tulips, azaleas and narcissi in the so-called pillar garden and a host of other varieties of flowers and plants. The park also contains an octagonal chapel with seven circular stained-glass windows showing the park's most beautiful flowers. It is here that McEachern was buried. The small building at the side of the villa holds a botanical library.

1

1) Gardens, Temple of Pan and Daphne
2) Gardens in full bloom

1

2

1) Gardens
2) The "cherub" fountain
3) Exterior view
4) "The fisher boy" by V. Gemito

3

PALLANZA

Pallanza stands on the northern edge of the Golfo Borromeo. This well-appointed tourist spot is subdivided into two parts: the upper part, la Villa, is considered to be the older of the two, although it has in fact been rebuilt. The lower, lakeside part, La Piazza, is mediaeval with its typical porticoes and narrow, twisting streets. Appointed royal court in 885, it was the only village of the Verbano region not to become part of the Borromeo feudal domain. Of interest are the Romanesque church of S. Stefano, built in the old village centre and rebuilt in the seventeenth century, and the sixteenth-century parish church of S. Leonardo, with its high lateral bell-tower, situated in the mediaeval part. Outstanding among the numerous eighteenth-century residences is Palazzo Viani-Dugnani, built in Baroque style in the late seventeenth century. It today houses the museum and landscape gallery, which exhibits works by Paolo Trubetzkoy, as well as archaeological finds and landscape paintings. The buildings along the lakeside testify to the development of tourism during the nineteenth century. Also of interest near Pallanza are the Romanesque church of S. Remigio, on the splendid promontory of Castagnola, and the Madonna di Campagna, a church with a Romanesque bell-tower and a cupola after the style of Bramante.

1) Piazza Garibaldi and church of S. Leonardo
2) Church of La Madonna di Campagna
3) Aerial view of Verbania Point and the island of S. Giovanni
4) Fountain in Piazza Garibaldi
5) Church of La Madonna di Campagna, altar
6) S. Bernardino di Chiaravalle exorcising a possessed woman: detail

4

6
7

ISOLA MADRE

1) Aerial view of island, with Palanza in the background
2) Entrance to Isola Madre

Pag. 52-53
3) Borromeo Chapel
4) Doll Room
5) Pope Room
6) Dining room
7) Family drawing room
8) Entrance to island
9) Indian peacocks in gardens
10) Azaleas in bloom, pheasants and peacocks

Isola Madre is so called because of its size: it is the largest of the Borromean Islands and is also the farthest from dry land. A fortified settlement, it belonged to the bishop of Novara until 1501, when it became Borromeo property. Two family members, Lancillotto and Renato, decided to abandon it as a defence post and turned it into a sumptuous residence. In order to make room for new constructions, all of the existing buildings were demolished, including the ancient sanctuary of S. Vittore - from which the place took its name. Borromeo dedicated the island to his wife and it was called Isola Renata until the eighteenth century. Although the ambitious project was never completed, what remains of it can be seen today in the building with the twin-loggia façade, the Borromeo mausoleum and the luxuriant gardens. The construction of the house began in about 1550 but was only completed in later centuries. The interior is sumptuously decorated with seventeenth and eighteenth century furniture, tapestries and paintings, including portraits of the Borromeo family. The building also houses a museum containing contemporary furnishings and porcelain, a collection of dolls from as early as the seventeenth century and the famous puppet theatre, dating from the mid-eighteenth century. However, the island's main attraction are the gardens which cover it almost entirely. These are full of rhododendrons, azaleas, camelias and other exotic plants, while pheasants, peacocks and other colourful birds live there in perfect freedom.

1

1) Lakeside view (partial)
2) Aerial view
3) Landing stage
4) Piazza D. Ranzoni
5) Typical alleyway
6) Intra-Laveno ferry

INTRA

Intra stands on alluvial land between the S. Bernardino and S. Giovanni rivers, over which stands a seventeenth-century stone bridge. It has been Lago Maggiore's main commercial and industrial centre since the eighteenth century. An ancient Romanesque town, it shows very little evidence of its mediaeval past (it is cited as a "castrum" around 1100) and its characteristics are predominantly modern. The mainly nineteenth-century buildings along the lakeside include the Palazzo delle Beccherie (1855) and the Palazzo della Civica Delegazione (eighteenth century), which look out over Piazza Ranzoni, the local administrative centre. Two roads lead off the square - Via S. Fabiano and Via S. Vittore. The former is lined with Baroque-style buildings decorated with granite portals and wrought iron balconies and leads to the circular-plan church of the same name (1630). Via S. Vittore, the town's main shopping street, is lined with seventeenth and eighteenth century buildings, also with granite portals, and leads to the cathedral of S. Vittore (1708-1752). Erected on the site of an ancient church and mentioned in documents around the year 1000, it has a façade built in 1830 and a characteristic copper cupola that stands out in the distance as you approach the lake. Not far away is the oratory of S. Giuseppe, built in Baroque style between the seventeenth and eighteenth centuries on the site of an earlier Romanesque church, and the oratory of S. Rocco, a sixteenth century building with a Neo-Classical façade. Excellent examples of Baroque civic architecture are to be seen in Palazzo Perretti, Palazzo Scaramuccia and the Town Hall.

1

2

3

4

5

6

1) Aerial panorama
2) Cannero Castles' ruins
3) Typical fishing boat at Cannero Castles'

CANNERO

Situated opposite Luino on the Piedmont side of the lake, this picturesque town is the site of the annual camelia show which takes place in early spring. The scenic beauty of Cannero, with its lakeside lined with villas, is perfectly matched by a mild climate that allows the cultivation of trees and plants more typical of warmer areas, such as citrus trees, bougainvillea and even certain tropical species. Opposite the small town are the three famous Malpaga castle islands. Fortified between the eleventh and thirteenth centuries, these were dominated in the fifteenth century by the Ghibelline Mazzarditi family, who tyrannized the local people until ousted by the Borromeos. This family then rebuilt the fortress today called Vitaliana on the two main islands and used it as a defence post.

3

S. ANNA

Immersed in the thick vegetation of the Val Cannobina stands the church of S. Anna, built around the mid-seventeenth century. This small building can only be reached by means of a difficult little road. The church is famous above all for its position and has the typical look of the area, with its pointed bell-tower, ornate façade and simple wooden portal. It stands close to the so-called Orrido di S. Anna, an extremely steep rocky gorge carved out by the waters of the river Cannobina over the centuries. The place is popular with tourists and offers an excellent view over the splendid natural environment of the Valle Cannobina, with its carpet of beech and chestnut trees.

CANNOBIO

Cannobio stands at the mouth of the Val Cannobina, the last Italian town on the western side of Lago Maggiore before the Swiss border. It is famous for its picturesque position (lying partly on the lakeside, partly in the valley) and for its particularly mild climate. Already inhabited during Roman times, it preserves a predominantly mediaeval appearance. At the far end of the lakeside part, lined with quaint little porticoed houses, stands the Santuario della Pietà. Work on it lasted from 1526 to 1533 and it was rebuilt by Carlo Borromeo in 1583. The Bramante-style lantern was added in the early seventeenth century, while the façade dates back to 1909. The Baroque-style interior houses a precious altar work by Gaudenzio Ferrari (the Ascent to Calvary) and numerous seventeenth and eighteenth century paintings. Another fine religious building is the collegiate church of S. Vittore, rebuilt in the eighteenth century on the foundations of a very ancient church that had been demolished at the end of the preceding century. The mediaeval Palazzo della Regione, also known as Palazzo Parrasio, was built with granite blocks between 1291 and 1294. Beneath the barrel vaults of its portico can be seen headstones and emblems dating back to the fourteenth century, as well as two Roman tombs. The so-called Torre del Comune stands at the side of the building. In fact it is a Romanesque stone bell-tower belonging to the old twelfth-century church of S. Vittore.

1

1) S.S. Pietà parchment in sanctuary of same name
2) Lakeside and landing stage (partial view)

Pag. 60-61
1) S.S. Pietà Sanctuary, interior decorations
2) S.S. Pietà Sanctuary, façade

2

2

BRISSAGO

1) Coat of arms
2) Parish church of SS. Pietro e Paolo (16th cent.), bell-tower
3) Brissago islands (or Isole dei "Conigli")
4) Lakeside
5) Landing stage
6) Panorama, with Ascona in the background

A famous resort on the western side of Lago Maggiore, Brissago lies in an area of rich vegetation, which is one of its main attractions. It was an independent republic throughout the Middle Ages and still enjoyed special autonomy at the end of the eighteenth century. The economy was given a remarkable boost in the middle of the nineteenth century by the foundation of the tobacco factory, which produced and still produces cigars and aromatic pipe tobacco. The consequent flourishing of the town is to be seen today in the numerous grand residences looking onto the lake. There is also a remarkable number of sixteenth-century style buildings - notably the parish church of S.S. Pietro e Paolo and the church of Madonna di Ponte. The parish church was built on a lakeside terrace surrounded by cypresses and was rebuilt in the early seventeenth century. It has a Baroque interior. Construction of the church of Madonna di Ponte began in 1528 and the building is considered to be the best example of Renaissance architecture in the Ticino canton. Of interest among the civic buildings is Palazzo Branca (Casa Baccalà), a Baroque construction dating from the mid-eighteenth century. A boat leaves from the lakeside for the Isole di Brissago (also called Isole dei "Conigli"). The largest of these islands, Isola S. Pancrazio, has a fine botanical park and an African museum. The remains of an ancient Romanesque church can be seen amidst the lush vegetation of Isola S. Appolinare.

VB
3763

1

ASCONA

Separated from Locarno by the river Maggia, Ascona is one of the liveliest and mo
elegant areas of Lago Maggiore. The picturesque lakeside is lined with centuries-old pla
trees, hotels, cafés and elegant shops which attract élite international tourism all ye
round. The town was once protected by three fortresses but has preserved hardly anythi
of its mediaeval appearance. The building most famous from an architectural point of vie
is the Casa Borroni (formerly Casa del Serodine). This sumptuous three-stor
seventeenth-century residence has a richly stuccoed façade (decorative strips and statue
the work of Giovan Battista Serodine, brother of the more famous Giovanni - a paint
whose altar-piece (1622) can be admired in the parish church of S.S. Pietro e Paolo. T
walls of the church of S. Maria della Misericordia, which has a splendid coffered ceilin
are decorated with fourteenth-sixteenth century frescoes. The Collegio Papio, which
annexed to the church, has an elegant two-tiered courtyard in late Renaissance sty
Ascona is not only famous for the highly professional music festivals organized there sin
1945 but also as an artistic and cultural centre. From the late nineteenth century it becar
popular with intellectuals and artists, who were particularly attracted to nearby Mor
Verità and the Eranos residence, situated at the foot of the mountain. The town contains
interesting museum of modern and contemporary art.

1) Harbour and S. Michele hill
2) General view
3) Characteristic view
4) Lakeside

4

1

LOCARNO

This important tourist centre is famous for its splendid position and its cultural activities (the international cinema festival and the flower show). Locarno was already inhabited during Roman times and, until the twelfth century, belonged to the diocese of Milan. It became the feudal domain of the Visconti in 1342 and of the Rusca family in 1439. It was taken by the Confederates in the early sixteenth century. The city castle (tenth century) was destroyed in 1156 by the Milanese when Locarno sided with Barbarossa against the Lombard cities, and again in 1513 by the Swiss. The restored building today holds a museum of contemporary art. Fifteenth-century frescoes are preserved in the church of S. Maria in Selva, which dates back to the fifteenth century and is now the cemetery chapel. The nearby church of S. Antonio was built in 1664 and reconstructed around 1860. It contains important eighteenth-century frescoes. The most important building in Locarno - the collegiate church of S. Vittore - is, on the other hand, of Romanesque origin (twelfth century) and preserves some of its original architecture. The sanctuary of the Madonna del Sasso is situated in a magnificent panoramic position to the north. Founded in 1487 and rebuilt in the early seventeenth century, it preserves an interior fresco by Bramantino (1522). Gravitating around Piazza Grande, Locarno has a wealth of seventeenth-eighteenth century buildings: worthy of particular mention are Casa Rusca, Casa Ranzoni and Casa dei Canonici (formerly Palazzo Orelli), while Casa del Negromante dates back to the mediaeval period.

1) Castle. Museum of Contemporary Art
2) Lakeside and landing stage
3) Piazza Grande
4) Gardens
5) Lake panorama
6) Sanctuary of the Madonna del Sasso
7) "The ecstacy of Christ" by A. Ciseri
8) Sanctuary of the Madonna del Sasso, interior
9) Wooden statue of the Madonna del Sasso

2

7
8
9

1) Cardada cable way
2) Cardada
3) Church of Magadino, organ
4) Vira Gambaragno
5) Camping sites at Tereno

4

5

MACCAGNO

Maccagno lies on the main road from Luino to the Swiss border. It is divided into Upper and Lower Maccagno by the river Giona and is a little over a kilometre from the opposite side of the lake. Lower Maccagno, which has existed since prehistoric times, retains an interesting mediaeval appearance, thanks to its narrow streets, stairways and picturesque vaults. The restored Zecca building (1662) stands in Piazza Roma: it was here that the town operated the money minting concession it obtained from the Mandelli family, who governed it for a long time. The square is dominated by the Torre Imperiale (twelfth-thirteenth century), situated on a rock from which there is a clear view from the Golfo Borromeo to Cannobio. Not far away along the same road is the sanctuary of the Madonna. It was built on a huge lakeside rock and is supported by massive arches. Beautiful late Gothic frescoes can be admired in the church of S. Antonio in Upper Maccagno.

1) Sanctuary, interior
2) General view

LUINO

A pleasant town situated near the mouth of the river Tresa, Luino lies in a wide bay sheltered by hills along the railway line connecting Italy and Switzerland.
Mentioned as early as the year 1100 as "Luvinum", the town was the scene of important events during the Risorgimento and is today an important industrial centre. The church of the Madonna del Carmine (fifteenth century), containing frescoes from the Luini school (1540), lies next to the remains of a Roman necropolis. The church of S. Giuseppe (eighteenth century) stands close to the cemetery, while the fifteenth-century church of S. Pietro (rebuilt in 1668) with its Romanesque bell-tower (eleventh century) houses a series of fifteenth and sixteenth-century frescoes, including an "Adoration of the Magi" attributed to Bernardino Luini. The central town square, Piazza Garibaldi, contains a monument to Garibaldi (1867) and is the site of a large picturesque market, which probably originated with an edict by Carlo V, proclaimed in 1541.

1

1) Church of S. Pietro in Campagna
2) Panorama
3) Harbour
4) Market

2

3

LAVENO

Probably of Roman origin (named after Titus Labenius, a Roman general), Laveno was Visconti feudal land before falling into the possession of the Sforza and, finally, the Borromeo family. It fell under Spanish dominion between 1535 and 1706 and was then ruled by Austria. It later became a well-known tourist location and ceramics manufacturing centre: the abandoned Richard Ginori Italian Ceramics Company still bears witness to this today. Although the town does not offer any particular attractions from an artistic point of view - apart from seventeenth and eighteenth century villas and houses - it lies in a remarkable setting in a small picturesque bay and is dominated by the Sasso del Ferro (1062 m), which can be reached in the "Poggio S. Elsa" cable car. From this point in particular, there is an excellent view over the Golfo Borromeo, Mottarone and, in the distance, Monte Rosa.

2

1) Harbour at Caldé
2) Lake from Poggio S. Elsa cable car
3) Harbour
4) View from lake; ferry

4

S. CATERINA DEL SASSO

Situated in a wonderful panoramic position overlooking the lake and offering an excellent view from the Golfo Borromeo to Angera, the charming sanctuary of S. Caterina del Sasso dates back to the thirteenth century. The earliest center, a small church dedicated to Santa Caterina d'Alessandria, is traditionally thought to have been built by Alberto da Besozzo - a merchant who became a hermit after having survived a shipwreck, the remains of which are preserved in the building. In 1230, the Dominican friars built a small convent and an oratory; around 1450 these were joined to the original church by Gothic and Renaissance arched galleries, thus creating a single sanctuary which was itself extended during the seventeenth century. A portico leads into the capitular room, containing thirteenth and fourteenth-century frescoes. Passing through a small courtyard, where you can admire a wine-press dating from 1759, there is another portico, whose walls bear what remains of a "danse macabre" fresco originally composed of fifteen episodes. The refectory houses a seventeenth-century Last Supper scene. The church has a Romanesque bell-tower and an entrance with four arches, and is home to sixteenth-century frescoes and seventeenth-century floral decorations. The church has been damaged by numerous landslides and restoration and consolidation work began in 1970. It again became an active place of worship in 1986.

1) Portico in Convent
2) Convent and Sanctuary of S. Caterina del Sasso

ISPRA

1) Panorama
2) Beach

Situated at the foot of Monte del Prete (313 m) and Monte Nassi (270 m), Ispra is a modern, well-appointed tourist centre and the headquarters of the EEC's Euratom Centre for Nuclear Studies (CCR). The town, which is mentioned as early as the ninth century, is the point of departure for the path leading up to the top of Monte del Prete, where you can admire the remains of the mediaeval castle of S. Cristoforo. At one time there was also a chapel dating back at least to the thirteenth century. In the ancient chapel situated behind the apse of the parish church of S. Martino (seventeenth century) some interesting frescoes are to be seen. The bell-tower of the church was constructed in 1680. Along the lakeside stand a number of nineteenth century villas (e.g. Villa Ranci Ortigiosa, Villa Saramosa Brivio) set amidst fine gardens. On the road leading out of the town is the Neo-Classical funeral monument (1865) to Contessa Antonietta Castelbarco Albani.

1

2

1) Aerial view of Rocca di Angera
2) Rocca di Angera, Chamber of Justice
3) Rocca di Angera from Arona

ANGERA

Situated opposite Arona on the south side of the lake, Angera lies in a small bay and is sheltered by the green and rocky hill on which the famous Fort Viscontea stands. The town was already a settlement in prehistoric times and began to gain importance in Roman times. This importance reached its height in the Middle Ages, when Angera's dominant position on the lake made it both a busy commercial centre and an important strategic site. It belonged to the archbishops of Milan until 1200 and then became part of the feudal domain of the Visconti, who were involved in a fierce struggle with the Torriani. It later passed into the hands of the Borromeo family (1449). The rich history of the town, whose characteristic narrow streets preserve its mediaeval appearance, is to be seen in the numerous prehistoric finds, as well as a rich collection of material from Roman times, housed in the local archeological museum in Palazzo Pretorio (sixteenth century). These were discovered in the local area and in the large necropolis near the present-day cemetery. The town stretches out towards the hill and down to the lakeside, which is lined with old chestnut trees. The sanctuary of the Madonna della Riva was built towards the middle of the seventeenth century. Its central-plan interior contains some remarkable fourteenth and

1

2

3

fifteenth-century frescoes. Isola di Partegora faces the lakeside in the centre of the small bay: this is surrounded by canebrakes and is a favourite spot for nature and lakeland lovers. The so-called Antro di Mitra, a cave that was certainly inhabited in prehistoric times, lies along the road leading from the town to the fortress. During the Roman period, it was used as a place of worship to the god Mitra, the protector of commerce (numerous finds from the area are kept in the museum).
The Fort dominating the town from the hilltop is the main attraction. First mentioned in 1060, the castle was enlarged and used as a fortification by the Visconti and was later transformed into a residence by the Borromeo family. The oldest part of the building is the Castellano tower. It dates back to pre-Visconti 1100. During later periods (fourteenth-seventeenth century), other parts were added, including the Visconti building and the Borromeo wing, on the town side. The first floor of the Visconti building is occupied by the large Chamber of Justice, whose large ogive vaults are decorated by a cycle of remarkable fifteenth-century frescoes, including the Sun and Saturn (part of a lost Zodiac Figuration), a Madonna with Saints and works celebrating Archbishop Ottone Visconti and his struggle with the Torriani family. Since 1988, the Fortress has housed the first and only Doll Museum in Italy. Visitors can admire the collection of Princess Bona Borromeo, with items from throughout Europe. Besides these valuable dolls, wooden and tin toys and miniature furniture make this museum unique in Europe.

1

1) Rocca di Angera at sunset
2-3) Two exhibits in the Museum of Dolls

2

3

INDEX

© Published by KINA ITALIA S.P.A. Milan
Printed by KINA ITALIA S.P.A. Milan
Sole Distributor for Italy: Muzio - Milan
Photographs: Aerfoto I. Buga, Enzo Ferri,
Maurilio Mazzola, Riccardo Rosnati, Renzo Sanbiagio,
Carlo Muzio, Mugnai
Pagination by: Renzo Matino